The Genius Of THE BENIN KINGDOM

INNOVATIONS FROM PAST CIVILIZATIONS

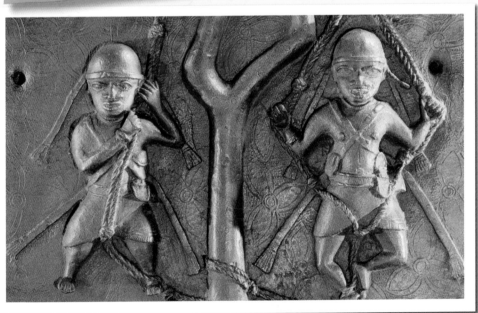

SONYA NEWLAND

CRABTREE
PUBLISHING COMPANY
WWW.CRABTREEBOOKS.COM

CRABTREE
PUBLISHING COMPANY
WWW.CRABTREEBOOKS.COM

Published in Canada
Crabtree Publishing
616 Welland Avenue
St. Catharines, ON
L2M 5V6

Published in the United States
Crabtree Publishing
PMB 59051
350 Fifth Ave, 59th Floor
New York, NY 10118

Published in 2020 by Crabtree Publishing Company

First published in Great Britain in 2019 by The Watts Publishing Group
Copyright © The Watts Publishing Group 2019

Author: Sonya Newland

Editorial director: Kathy Middleton

Editors: Sonya Newland, Petrice Custance

Proofreader: Melissa Boyce

Series Designer: Rocket Design (East Anglia) Ltd

Designer: Steve Mead

Prepress technician: Tammy McGarr

Print coordinator: Katherine Berti

Consultant: Philip Parker

Printed in the U.S.A./072019/CG20190501

Photo credits:
Alamy: Heritage Image Partnership Ltd cover, 9, age footstock 3t, 24, 25, UniversalImagesGroup 3b, 22, 26, The History Collection 6, Adam Eastland 7t, UniversalImagesGroup 8, Lanmas 11, Granger Historical Picture Archive 13, Werner Forman/Universal Images 15, The Picture Art Collection 16, Lebrecht Music & Arts 19t, Peter Horree 21, Artokoloro Quint Lox Limited 28; Ron Dixon: 4; Getty Images: Werner Forman 1, 5t, 12, 14, 17, 18, 20r, 27, 29, Print Collector 5b, DEA / A. DAGLI ORTI 10, PIUS UTOMI EKPEI 23b; Shutterstock: Julia_Lelija 7b, Seashell World 19b, Boulenger Xavier 20l, Ilia Torlin 23t, Keith Gentry 23b.

All design elements from Shutterstock.

Every attempt has been made to clear copyright. Should there be any inadvertent omission please apply to the publisher for rectification.

The website addresses (URLs) included in this book were valid at the time of going to press. However, it is possible that contents or addresses may have changed since the publication of this book. No responsibility for any such changes can be accepted by either the author or the Publisher.

Library and Archives Canada Cataloguing in Publication

Title: The genius of the Benin Kingdom / Sonia Newland.
Names: Newland, Sonya, author.
Series: Genius of the ancients.
Description: Series statement: The genius of the ancients |
  Includes index.
Identifiers: Canadiana (print) 20190108371 |
  Canadiana (ebook) 20190108401 |
  ISBN 9780778765943 (softcover) |
  ISBN 9780778765745 (hardcover) |
  ISBN 9781427123916 (HTML)
Subjects: LCSH: Benin (Kingdom)—Civilization—Juvenile literature. |
  LCSH: Technological innovations—Nigeria—Benin (Kingdom)—
  Juvenile literature. | LCSH: Benin (Kingdom)—History—
  Juvenile literature. | LCSH: Benin (Kingdom)—Kings and rulers—
  Juvenile literature.
Classification: LCC DT515.9.B37 N49 2019 | DDC j966.9/301—dc23

Library of Congress Cataloging-in-Publication Data

CIP available at the Library of Congress

CONTENTS

THE BENIN KINGDOM

Where and when?

The Benin Kingdom began around 900 C.E., when the Edo peoples of West Africa settled in the **rain forests** of what is now Nigeria. At the beginning of this **civilization**, the Edo lived in many separate villages. Over time, these communities grew to form a strong and united kingdom the Edo called Igodomigodo.

The first kings were called Ogisos. This period of Ogiso rule is known as the first **dynasty** of the kingdom. The Ogisos lost power around 1180. After a brief period without kings, a second dynasty began. The new rulers were called Obas. Igodomigodo then became known as the Benin Kingdom.

This map shows the Benin Kingdom as well as some of the surrounding kingdoms.

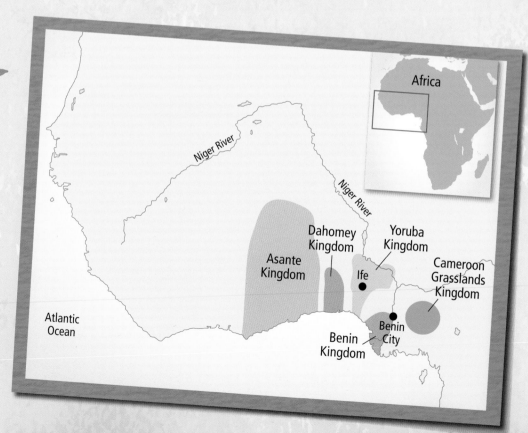

Benin at its height

Under the Obas, Benin became a wealthy and successful empire, centered on its great capital, Benin City. The Edo people enjoyed successful trading relationships with other African kingdoms and, later, with several European countries. For 200 years, a series of strong warrior kings kept their citizens safe and protected the empire from attack by neighboring kingdoms.

What happened?

In the 1600s, after a succession of weak Obas, the kingdom began to decline. By the 1800s, Benin was no longer the great empire it had once been. This made it an easy target for greedy outsiders. The British wanted access to Benin's **natural resources**, such as rubber and palm oil. In 1897, the British invaded the Benin Kingdom and burned Benin City to the ground. Benin then became part of the British Empire.

The people of Benin became famous for their works of art. The Benin Bronzes are a series of sculptures and plaques from Benin's royal palace that were taken by the British.

A British invasion in 1897 ended the Kingdom of Benin.

5

WARRIOR KINGS

The Benin Kingdom's greatest asset was its strong leaders, or Obas. Under a series of five great warrior kings, the empire grew to its greatest size and power.

GENIUS
★ FIVE GREAT OBAS ★

From Ogiso to Oba

The Ogisos ruled the early Benin Kingdom until the 1100s. Then, the Ogisos grew weak and began to lose control of the kingdom. The leaders of different villages began to fight one another. To help restore peace, the Edo people asked a prince from Ife, in the nearby Yoruba Kingdom, to help. The prince's son, Eweka, established the second dynasty in the Benin Kingdom—the rule of the Obas.

This painting from the 1600s shows an Oba on his horse in a procession. The king played an important part in Edo **rituals** and celebrations.

Ewuare the Great

The first of the five great warrior Obas, Ewuare, came to the throne around 1440. During his 40-year reign, Benin became a strong and powerful kingdom. Ewuare began trading with Portuguese merchants, which made the kingdom wealthy. It also enabled the Oba to pay for a large army. In turn, the army conquered new territory and expanded the Benin Kingdom.

Building the Edo empire

Ewuare's son, Ozolua, was a great soldier who won many battles and extended the kingdom even further. The next Oba, Esigie, was responsible for expanding the kingdom to the east, including conquering parts of the Yoruba Kingdom.

The empire reached its greatest size under Oba Orhogbua. By the end of his reign, Benin stretched beyond the Niger River and west to what is now Ghana. The fifth great warrior king was Ehengbuda. Despite threats by **rebellious** local **chieftains**, he was strong enough to keep control of the empire. After his death in about 1601, however, the Benin Kingdom began to decline.

This brass plaque from the Oba's palace is believed to show the warrior king Ozolua.

The Edo believed an ancient king of Benin wrestled the god Olokun and won, earning him the right to wear **coral**.

TEST OF TIME

Although the British conquered Benin in 1897, the Obas remained the spiritual leaders of the Edo people. There are still Obas in Nigeria today, and they play an important part in Edo **culture** and traditions.

THE POWER OF THE OBA

The Oba had control over almost everything within the Benin Kingdom. He owned all the land and decided what it should be used for.

A life of luxury

The Oba lived in a grand palace in the heart of Benin City. Hundreds of people lived at this **court**, making sure the Oba had everything he wanted. The Oba had several wives and many children, so a large staff was needed to take care of him and his family.

WOW!

The Oba's mother, known as Iyoba, or queen mother, was also an important figure in Edo **society**. She was said to have special powers. She was not allowed to see her son after he became Oba, in case she tried to use magic to control him!

This ivory pendant shows an Iyoba, or mother of the Oba. It may be Idia, wife of Oba Ozolua and mother of Oba Esigie.

Honoring the Oba

The Oba was treated as a god, and was respected and **revered** by the Edo people. In the presence of the Oba, ordinary people had to remain kneeling. They were not allowed to look directly at him. The Oba himself was thought to have magic powers, and special festivals were held every year to renew his powers.

Keeping control

The first Oba, Ewuare, established a system of town chiefs, who could report on what happened in the provinces of Benin. As time passed, the Oba employed even more advisers so he would know what was happening all across his kingdom. The Uzama, or elders, were the most important. Other advisers came from villages outside the city. They had many different jobs, such as farmers, soldiers, or craftspeople, so they could advise the Oba on different things.

Benin art often showed animals that represented the Oba's powers. These two ivory leopards were placed on either side of his throne during ceremonies.

SOCIAL HIERARCHY

There was a strict **hierarchy** to society in the Benin Kingdom. The Oba was at the top. Below him were members of his family and **nobles**, while ordinary people were at the lowest level. According to Europeans who visited Benin, no matter what level in society, everyone in Benin lived comfortably.

Forgive and forget

In Benin City, there were captains who acted as judges when people disagreed with one another. The justice system was based on forgiveness. If someone was found guilty of stealing, they could apologize and return or replace the goods. If they did so, they would not be punished. When Europeans first arrived in Benin City, they were amazed at how little crime there was.

This picture shows a scene of daily life in Benin City, with the Oba's palace at the heart of the city.

Daily life

The Europeans were surprised at how happy even the most ordinary Edo people seemed to be. There were no homeless or hungry people. The streets were wide and clean, and the houses were large and well-maintained. Every house had its own well to provide the family with fresh water. Visitors reported that Benin City was so free from crime that many of the houses had doorways but no actual doors!

The slave trade

However, not everyone in Benin had a happy life. Traders bought and sold enslaved people in Benin. These people were usually taken from lands conquered by the Edo, then sold to other parts of Africa. Some enslaved people remained in Benin to work for noblemen who lived there. After Europeans made contact with Benin, they began purchasing and trading enslaved people as well. At first, most enslaved people were women. By 1700, men were also being bought and sold.

TEST OF TIME

The Edo left no written records, so it is difficult to know what life was really like for ordinary people. What we know about the Benin Kingdom today comes from reports by Europeans who visited Benin City, and from the art of the Edo people that survives today.

Traders would bid to purchase enslaved people at markets.

RELIGION

The people of Benin worshiped many gods and goddesses. The festivals held to honor them were an important part of life in the kingdom.

Gods of the Edo people

Osanobua is the creator god in the Edo religion, or the god who is believed to have made the world. The word Osanobua means god in the Edo language. Osanobua's children became the main gods worshiped by the Edo people. His son, Olokun, was ruler of the oceans. He was also thought to bring wealth and **fertility** to the land.

Osanobua's daughter, Obiemven, was the goddess of childbirth and farming. Another of Osanobua's sons, Ogiuwu, was the god of death.

WOW!

Religion in the Benin Kingdom involved the practice of human **sacrifice**. When an Oba died, it was considered an honor for his closest friends and ministers to be killed and buried with their leader.

This plaque shows two men performing a ritual at a festival. They are using ropes in a special dance to honor the god of war, Ogun.

The spirit world

The Edo people believed the universe was divided into two regions—the everyday world and the spirit world. The gods and **ancestors** lived in the spirit world, but they could affect the lives of people in the everyday world. The Edo also thought that powerful humans, such as **witch doctors**, could talk to the gods and use their power to heal the sick.

Celebrating festivals

Religious festivals were held throughout the year to honor the gods and the Oba. Festivals also marked important seasonal events, such as **harvest** time. Everyone contributed to the festival in some way, whether by growing food for the feasts or by making costumes for the parades and celebrations.

TEST OF TIME

Some **traditional** ceremonies to honor the gods are still held by the Edo people today, such as the festival of Igue, which takes place at the end of each year. The festival is believed to bring good luck to the Oba and his people.

The Oba always attended festivals in Benin City. In this picture, the Oba (shown on a horse) leads a procession of musicians during a festival.

13

PROFESSIONAL SOLDIERS

GENIUS ★ WELL-TRAINED ARMY ★

To build and control his empire, the Oba needed a strong and **disciplined** fighting force. Obas Ozolua and Esigie created huge armies—and often put them to use.

The commander in chief

The Oba was the head of the army. He had his own royal **regiment**, and these handpicked men served as his personal bodyguards as well as soldiers. The Oba decided when the kingdom should go to war, and he worked with military commanders to plan battles. Some Obas even led their armies into battle.

This statue shows a Benin warrior on horseback.

14

Structure of the army

The Benin army was very well organized. The Oba relied on a **network** of commanders including the Iyase, the commander of the army regiments in the city. However, men from all over the kingdom served in the army. Groups from villages beyond the city walls formed the backbone of the fighting force. They answered immediately when the Oba called them to arms. They carried handmade shields crafted from wood and animal skins.

Weapons of war

At first, most soldiers fought with swords and spears made of brass and iron, as well as wooden crossbows. In the 1400s, Portuguese traders arrived in Benin with weapons the Edo had never seen before—guns. Because the Benin people were not Christians, the Portuguese refused to sell them guns. However, some Portuguese joined the Benin army as paid soldiers and used guns against the Edo's enemies. It was not until the 1690s that Dutch traders started selling guns to Benin.

This plaque from the Oba's palace shows a Portuguese soldier with a gun called a matchlock.

WOW!

Oba Ozolua was a famous soldier. It is said that he won around 200 battles—a record that earned him the nickname "Ozolua the Conqueror."

DESIGN AND ENGINEERING

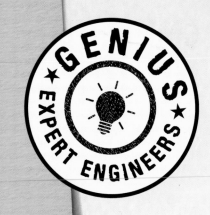

GENIUS
★ EXPERT ENGINEERS ★

The Edo people were geniuses at town planning and **engineering**. The construction of Benin City was one of their greatest achievements.

Original Benin City

There were small villages scattered all across the Benin Kingdom, but most of the population was concentrated in Benin City. Almost nothing of the city remains today, as it was burned to the ground by the British in 1897. Most of what we know about Benin City comes from written accounts by Europeans who visited it beginning in the 1400s.

A grand plan

The European visitors were impressed by Benin City. They remarked on how well it was planned and designed, and described it as grand and clean. The visitors also wrote about strongly built clay houses that lined long, straight streets. Benin City was one of the first cities to have streetlights. Large metal lamps were lit at night using palm oil.

Benin City was designed as a grid of long, straight streets.

City defenses

To keep the capital city safe from attack, it was surrounded by deep ditches in the north and huge walls in the south. The walls of Benin City were an engineering **marvel**.

Built between 800 and 1500, the walls covered more than 620 miles (1,000 km). They were the largest **earthwork** structure in the world. Although none of the city walls remain, experts think the walls may have been four times as long as the Great Wall of China.

WOW!

The outer settlement walls were built by ordinary men and women, not construction workers. It is estimated that it took 150 million hours of digging to lay the foundations for the walls.

Only a few of the ancient earthworks and ditches that surrounded the old city can still be seen.

ditch

earthwork

TRADE

Trade was essential to the success of the Benin Kingdom, bringing wealth and power to the Oba and his people. Trading was considered an important profession.

GENIUS ★ THRIVING ECONOMY ★

Neighborly trade

As the Benin Kingdom grew under the rule of the Obas, the Benin people came into contact with other African peoples and began trading with them. The Niger River (see map on page 4) to the north of Benin City provided a perfect trade route. Goods could be easily transported to nearby African kingdoms along the river.

(((BRAIN WAVE)))

The Edo people wanted to show their strength against cheats and thieves. If a foreign trader stole from a Benin trader, no one from Benin would trade with anyone from the same region or country as the thieving trader until they had apologized and returned the goods.

Portuguese traders such as the ones shown on this plaque were the first Europeans to visit Benin.

Overseas traders

Later, the Atlantic Ocean to the south opened up the kingdom to trade with European countries. The first Portuguese merchant ships arrived in 1485 and, later, the Dutch, British, French, and Spanish all came to trade with the Benin Kingdom. These foreign merchants were not allowed in Benin villages. Instead, they would meet at an agreed location to carry out their trade there. Sometimes negotiations between the two sides would last for weeks!

Goods for sale

Trade in Africa did not involve money. Instead, people traded goods for other things that they wanted. The people of Benin valued foreign items, such as brass bracelets from Europe, which they could melt down and use in their own metalworking. They also bought luxury items such as coral and cloth. In exchange, Benin traders offered goods including ivory from elephant tusks and food such as peppercorns, which were very popular in Europe.

This carved ivory saltcellar from the 1600s shows European traders and their ship.

WOW!

Cowrie shells were a highly prized item in the Benin Kingdom. They were used as a form of money, and each Oba would display his collection of shells as a show of wealth.

European traders often arrived loaded with cowrie shells to trade with the Benin people.

FARMING

Crops were important to the Benin Kingdom. They helped feed the population and they also produced valuable trading goods. Farming was a respected profession among the Edo people.

GENIUS
EFFICIENT AGRICULTURE

Crops and livestock

Farmers lived in villages outside Benin City. They cleared nearby areas of rain forest to grow crops. The main crop was yams, but farmers also grew beans, rice, peanuts, millet, sorghum, onions, and cotton. They grew pepper too, which was much sought-after by European traders. Villagers raised livestock such as sheep, goats, and cattle for food.

This plaque shows a servant collecting fruit. Mango, papaya, and other tropical fruits were common in the Benin Kingdom.

Yams, a type of sweet potato, were the **staple** crop in the Benin Kingdom. Ordinary people probably ate them at every meal. Yams are still a staple of the local diet today.

Division of labor

The people in a village all shared responsibility for the surrounding farmland. In farming villages, men **sowed**, tended, and harvested the main crops such as yams. The men worked together with friends and relatives to make sure there was a good harvest. Women were in charge of the less important crops such as onions, which were grown in smaller areas. Women were also responsible for selling farm produce in the markets.

Hunting and fishing

Wild animals, such as deer and antelope, lived in the rain forests. The men would hunt wild animals with bows and arrows, then cook them for meat. Larger animals, such as elephants and leopards, also lived in the forests. But only a few men were given permission by the Oba to hunt them for their ivory and skins.

TEST OF TIME

In ancient times, the Oba owned all the land and decided how it could be used. Today, the ruler of the Edo people still officially owns the land in this part of Nigeria, but does not make any decisions about its use.

This ivory figure from the 1600s shows a woman from the Benin Kingdom.

THE ART OF BENIN

GENIUS ★ **ARTS AND CRAFTS**

The Benin Kingdom is best known for its amazing art. Artists and craftspeople were skilled in all different types of art. They worked in many different materials, from clay and wood to precious metal and ivory.

Masks of the gods

Carved wooden masks from the Benin Kingdom show amazing skill and **artistry**. They were often made for special ceremonies to honor the Oba. Because of this, many masks took the shape of animals such as leopards, which represented the king. The crocodile was also an important animal in Benin culture, representing the Oba's swift justice against those who opposed him.

Coral and ivory

Coral was believed to be a gift from the sea god Olokun, so it was very valuable in Benin culture. Craftspeople made beautiful jewelry from coral, such as necklaces and bracelets. Ivory was also a precious material. Because it came from elephant tusks, it was a symbol of strength and purity. Only the Oba and a few important chiefs were allowed to wear jewelry that had been carved from ivory.

Leopards were considered the king of animals, so they were a common symbol of the Oba's power in Benin art.

Village crafts

In the villages outside Benin City, craftspeople created practical items such as clay pots and bowls. There were also **blacksmiths** who made tools and weapons for others in their village. **Weavers** created fabrics out of cotton fibers. The fabrics were often created in colorful striped patterns, using dye made from plant **extracts**. Fabrics were traded with people from other African kingdoms and tribes.

cotton plant

WOW!

The Edo people may have invented the African instrument called the thumb piano, or mbira. This is a small wooden board fitted with metal keys that play different notes when they are plucked.

thumb piano

Some traditional pieces are still used today. This carved ivory tusk is being blown to mark the **coronation** of the new Oba.

CRAFT GUILDS

★GENIUS★
SPECIALIZED PROFESSIONS

A guild is a group of workers practicing the same trade. In the Benin Kingdom, members of a guild lived and worked together. They helped and supported each other to make sure they all created excellent work.

Ere's idea

The guild system was established in the Benin Kingdom during the rule of the Ogisos. Ogiso Ere came to the throne in about 16 C.E. and ruled for 60 years. During that time, trade with neighboring tribes increased and there was a great demand for arts and crafts. Ere decided to organize his workers into guilds, believing that this would guarantee the highest standards. He wanted Benin art to be considered the best.

This bracelet shows mudfish. The mudfish was considered special by the Edo because it can breathe both on land and underwater.

24

Guilds for everything

At the height of the kingdom, under the great warrior Obas, there were more than 40 guilds in Benin City. There were guilds for wood carvers, ivory carvers, weavers, leatherworkers, blacksmiths, and many other artists and craftspeople. Each guild had a special job to perform for the Oba. The most famous and important guild was the brass casters' guild (see pages 26 to 27).

Grand designs

Within the guilds, the craftspeople competed to make the most beautiful and eye-catching pieces they could. They would come up with their own designs intended to please the Oba. They believed that these designs were inspired by the gods and the spirits of their ancestors.

WOW!

It was not only craftspeople who belonged to guilds in ancient Benin society. There were also guilds for doctors, leopard hunters, acrobats, and dancers—all professions that the Oba valued.

This sculpture is called an ikegobo, which means altars to the hand. Ikegobo were made to honor individuals. This one is for Ehenua, a military commander.

TEST OF TIME

There are still craft guilds in Benin City today. They continue to make beautiful objects for the Oba, but now they also make them to sell to locals and visitors.

BENIN BRASS

From the time of Ogiso rule, the Edo people produced impressive metalwork. The Oba's palace was filled with brass plaques, masks, and statues.

The brass casters' guild

Brass is an **alloy** of the metals copper and zinc. It can be used to make practical objects, such as plates and bowls, but it can also be shaped into works of art. Brass casters were the most highly skilled and greatly admired workers in the Benin Kingdom. They were so important that they were only allowed to work for the Oba, and everything they made belonged to him.

Brass casters still work in Benin City today, creating art in the way the Edo have done for centuries.

The power of brass

People believed that brass had magical powers and could **ward** off evil. Because of this, the Oba surrounded himself with brass objects. These pieces showed Obas and other important people, as well as scenes from famous battles and other historical events. When the British invaded, they took more than 1,000 of these Benin Bronzes from the palace. Many can still be seen in the British Museum in London.

Casting brass

Craftspeople used a process called lost-wax casting to make these beautiful artworks. First, they created a model of the piece out of wax. This was buried in sand and then heated so that the wax melted into the sand, leaving a hollow **mold**. The brass was made by melting down copper and mixing it with melted tin. The liquid was poured into the mold and left to cool. Then the mold was broken open to reveal the piece, which was polished to a high shine and presented to the Oba.

WOW!

For religious reasons, women were not allowed to be metalworkers. In fact, they were not allowed to touch metal at all. Women were only allowed to be members of the weavers' guild.

This brass head was made using the lost-wax method. It may represent the sea god, Olokun.

MEDICINE

Medicine in the Benin Kingdom was a mixture of religion and **herbalism**. The Edo put their faith in witch doctors and people who knew about herbs.

The wrath of the gods

People in ancient Benin believed that illness could be caused by the anger of the gods or ancestors. If someone committed a crime, they might risk the **wrath** of the gods. And if people did not honor their ancestors in the right way, it was believed that these spirits might take revenge by inflicting a serious illness on them.

Diseases from overseas

When European traders first arrived in Benin, they brought with them diseases such as **smallpox**. The Edo had never been exposed to such foreign diseases before. They did not know what they were and had no idea how to treat them. They thought it must be a punishment from the gods.

This medicine vessel is in the shape of a figure. It is made of brass with a bead on top that may be made of coral. This suggests that it belonged in the court of the Oba.

Natural medicines

The people of ancient Benin knew that some plants could ease certain **ailments**. The rain forests they lived in had many healing plants. The Edo grew herbs for use in cooking and to help heal wounds. The god of medicine and healing was Osun. The Edo also used the word osun to describe the power of plants and herbs to heal and cure.

(((BRAIN WAVE)))

As they had no way of writing things down, Edo elders passed on knowledge orally. Every evening, villagers would gather around a campfire and listen to storytellers. They told tales about the history of the Edo people, the founding of the Benin Kingdom, and **myths** about the gods. Storytellers also passed on important and practical knowledge, such as herbal cures.

This pendant would have been worn during rituals to honor the god Osun. It was a symbol of the Oba's link with the magic power of herbs.

GLOSSARY

ailment A minor illness

alloy A mixture of two metals

ancestor A family member who lived long ago

artistry The skill that goes into creating art

blacksmith Someone who makes objects from iron or steel

chieftain The leader of a tribe

civilization The stage of a human society, such as its culture and way of life

coral A hard pink material made from a sea animal

coronation A ceremony during which a sovereign is crowned

court The home and the people who work for a sovereign

culture The beliefs and customs of a group of people

disciplined Describes someone who strictly follows rules

dynasty A line of rulers who inherited the throne from one another

earthwork Soil piled to create a protective hill

engineering The design and building of machines and structures

extract The juice or liquid removed from a plant

fertility The ability to produce children

harvest To gather a crop

herbalism The use of herbs to treat illnesses

hierarchy A system in which things are organized according to their importance

marvel Something that causes curiosity or awe

mold A frame that gives shape to something

myth An invented story related to history

natural resources Materials or substances from nature that can be used to earn money

network A system of connected departments working together

noble To have a high rank or title

rain forest A tropical forest in an area with high rainfall

rebellious Describes someone who acts against authority

regiment A group of armed forces

revered To be respected with awe

ritual A religious ceremony in which actions are performed in a particular order

sacrifice When a living thing is killed to please the gods

smallpox A contagious disease

society A group of people living together in a community

sowed Planted or scattered seeds

staple Something that is basic or necessary

traditional Describes beliefs or customs that have existed for a long time

ward To guard or protect

weaver A person who creates fabrics by crossing threads together

witch doctor A member of a tribe who is believed to have healing powers and is able to communicate with gods and ancestors

wrath Violent anger

TIMELINE

900s	Edo people settle in the rain forests of West Africa.
1180	Ogisos lose power, leading to about 20 years with no ruler, followed by the second dynasty of the Obas.
1440	Ewuare becomes Oba—the first of the five great warrior kings.
1450	Work is completed on the walls of Benin City.
1485	Portuguese traders arrive in Benin.
1601	Ehengbuda dies—the last of the great warrior Obas.
1897	The British invade Benin and make it a colony of Britain.

INDEX

LEARNING MORE

Websites

www.bbc.com/bitesize/articles/z84fvcw

www.ks2history.com/benin-guide

Books

Howell, Izzi. *Benin (Explore!)*. Wayland, 2017.

Mason, Paul. *Daily Life in Ancient Benin*. Heinemann, 2015.

Richardson, Hazel. *Life in Ancient Africa*. Crabtree Publishing, 2005.